MUTUAL AID AND SELF-HELP

Coping strategies for excluded communities

Danny Burns and Marilyn Taylor

The POLICY PRESS

First published in Great Britain in 1998 by

The Policy Press
University of Bristol
Rodney Lodge
Grange Road
Bristol BS8 4EA
UK

Tel   +44 (0)117 973 8797
Fax   +44 (0)117 973 7308
E-mail tpp@bristol.ac.uk
Website http://www.bristol.ac.uk/Publications/TPP

In association with the Joseph Rowntree Foundation

ISBN 1 86134 122 9

Front cover: Photograph supplied by kind permission of Mark Simmons Photography, Bristol.

Danny Burns is Lecturer in Urban Policy, School for Policy Studies, University of Bristol and **Marilyn Taylor** is Professor in Social Policy at the University of Brighton.

The **Joseph Rowntree Foundation** has supported this project as part of its programme of research and innovative development projects, which it hopes will be of value to policy makers and practitioners. The facts presented and the views expressed in this report, however, are those of the authors and not necessarily those of the Foundation.

Cover design by Qube Design Associates, Bristol.

Printed in Great Britain by Hobbs the Printers Ltd, Southampton.

Contents

Contents

ONE

Introduction

The days when people could depend on the state to look after them from 'cradle to grave' are over. After a decade or more of privatisation inspired by the Thatcherite revolution, the new Labour government is exploring further shifts of responsibility for welfare and security from the state to individuals and communities. A wholesale restructuring of the benefits system has been promised; parents are to be made responsible in law for the actions of their children; and, as people survive longer into old age and expectations rise more generally, it seems inevitable that services available under the NHS will be increasingly rationed with people expected to make their own financial and other arrangements for future care.

Both Thatcherism and new Labour initiatives are a response to the economic stresses on the welfare state and appear to have much in common in their expectations of efficiency and self-sufficiency. But where Thatcherism was rooted in an anti-state, individualist libertarianism, new Labour's initiatives refer to a 'communitarian' philosophy which stresses mutual aid and a new kind of collective responsibility that no longer implies the intervention of the state.

Self-help and mutual aid are seen to offer solutions to a number of problems faced by policy makers today. Firstly, in the face of rising demands on the welfare budget, support networks have the potential to take the load off formal caring systems. Secondly, they are seen as a counterbalance to an apparent breakdown in social cohesion and as a way of re-establishing moral and social responsibilities eroded, first by dependency on the state and then by the individualism of the market. Thirdly, informal economic activities – skills exchanges, local exchange trading schemes (LETS) and similar schemes – have the potential to cushion the impact of poverty and perhaps to give those who have fallen to the margins of the labour market a step back into the mainstream.

Self-help and mutual aid have always been an important way for individuals to cope with immediate needs, with poverty and with social exclusion. In many circumstances and for many needs and activities, using formal services or joining a formal organisation may be a last, rather than a first resort. Thus, for many people on the margins of society, the welfare state only ever offered the means for bare survival (not even that in some cases); alternative ways of coping have been essential. Informal support systems have been the major source of social care for large parts of the population, while security and a sense of safety may be achieved as much by informal arrangements between friends and neighbours as by formal policing. Over the centuries, mutual aid has been particularly important for successive immigrant communities and for women, both for cultural reasons but also because of exclusion from more formal systems.

To acknowledge the importance of self-help and mutual aid is one thing, however. To rely on them as an instrument of policy is quite another. To do this, we need a much sharper understanding of the conditions which encourage self-help and mutual aid than has been evident in the policy debate so far, and a much more rigorous assessment of the capacity of such activity to move into the spaces implied by current policy shifts. As Mulgan and Landry argue, to see mutual help as a general solution to the problems caused by dependence on large corporate and government systems is to ignore its ephemeral nature and the limitations of time and resource that characterise involvement in such activity.

We have learnt quite a lot about different forms of mutual aid and self-help in recent years. Research on neighbourhood care and self-help groups, LETS and allotments, neighbourhood safety and D-I-Y indicates that this grouping of activities is extensive. In November 1997, *The Guardian* newsreport reported that there are now over 400 LETS schemes in the UK; a recent report from the Joseph Rowntree Foundation (Davidson et al, 1997) showed that DIY represented about 30% of the total value of all major work carried out between 1987 and 1991. The vast majority of care (of children, elderly people, sick people) is carried out by friends and relatives. Most leisure activities are informally organised by the participants.

But while it is relatively straightforward to identify activities associated with self-help and mutual aid, there is little clarity about what lies behind this apparently disparate set of activities and what distinguishes them from more institutional forms of social organisation. Despite the claims made for these activities, the dynamics which motivate and sustain them are poorly understood and the tensions and ambiguities which surround them are ignored by policies which, while welcoming their caring potential, are ambivalent about their legal status and their alternative economic solutions. Will the morality of those excluded from the mainstream be compatible with the rest of society? Can informal mutual aid survive the attentions and intentions of outside agencies? Will informal economic activities act as a step up or will they trap participants in ghettoised subsistence economies for the poor on the one hand, or criminal economies on the other?

This essay explores the potential and the limits of self-help and mutual aid. It begins in Chapter 2 by defining self-help and mutual aid in relation to other organised activity. Chapter 3 reviews what has been written about self-help and mutual aid in different communities. Chapters 4 and 5 explore the tensions between expectations of mutual aid networks and their reality, asking whether and in what circumstances these networks can be seen as a foundation for more formal engagement with the mainstream, or whether they act as an alternative to, or even reaction against it. Chapters 6 and 7 conclude by asking what the implications are for policy and practice in relation to excluded communities.

TWO

Mapping the territory

We define self-help as activity carried out by individuals for themselves or their families. Mutual aid involves reciprocal activity. What distinguishes these activities from other forms of social organisation is they are carried out *directly* by people. By this we mean that the activities draw directly on people's *own* labour power, skills and knowledge, and are neither mediated by or dependent upon any third party (although in certain cases they can be facilitated or supported by a third party). Specifically they are not dependent on either the state or the market. In this sense mutual aid is quite different from both the formal mutualism of guilds and building societies, and the proposals for personalised insurance plans which Frank Field has described as 'self-help' (Field, 1996).

Our definition of mutual aid is close to Rob Paton's 1989 definition of "the natural economy", which is based on a "logic of affinity expressed through informality, mutuality and voluntarism". We believe that there are a number of *organisational* characteristics which distinguish mutual aid and self-help from other socioeconomic forms of organisation. These are the extent to which forms of organisation are:

- professionalised (in the sense that they are run by paid workers);
- formally defined by the state;
- have representative or direct decision-making structures;
- take on an organisational or network structure.

Confining ourselves to non-profit organisations[1], five main categories of organisation can be distinguished by reference to these four organisational criteria. These are: the state, the voluntary/non-profit sector, the community sector, the sphere of informal mutual aid, and the sphere of personal and family activity. However, it is impossible to draw harsh boundary lines between each category. Firstly, no typology of this kind represents a perfect fit – there are organisations which do not sit happily with this broad categorisation. Secondly, this has to be seen as a dynamic spectrum of activity – organisations move up and down this list, on the one hand in response to growth and formalisation, on the other in response to demands for decentralisation and autonomy at local level. For these reasons, we have also sketched in the characteristics of the zones in between each of the main categories.

Figure 1 (p 7) shows the key organisational characteristics of each category[2]. The substantive focus of this report is on the four bands at the bottom of the diagram (black text on white background), but it is important to define them in direct relation to the formal sectors which are more commonly identified (white text on black background). It is to these that we turn first.

The organisations of *the state (a)* are large bureaucracies. They are professionally run and are required by law to provide certain services and carry out certain functions. They are normally accountable to committees of councillors or Members of Parliament elected by the voting public, or to appointees of the state.

The privatisation of services previously provided by the state has created a band of organisations which lie *between the state* and what has traditionally been thought of as *the voluntary sector (b)*. The organisations tend to be tightly regulated statutory bodies such as The Housing Corporation. Such organisations might include housing associations and 'floated off' not-for-profit trusts providing community care. They can be distinguished from the state sector by the type of decision-making structure that they have. Staff are responsible to a committee, but this will not be subject to appointment by the state. It is likely to be appointed by founders or incumbent trustees, reflecting professional or specialist expertise.

The voluntary sector (c) can be distinguished from this intermediary group because while its organisations are legally constituted they are less tightly regulated[3]. Unlike housing associations which are monitored on financial performance, policy and practice (eg, allocations policy), the regulation of charities is confined to setting boundaries to the type of activities which can be carried out and ensuring financial probity in the interests of the donors[4]. Less regulated still are non-charitable non-profit-distributing organisations, for example, those which engage in advocacy or campaigning services which are not deemed charitable. These simply have to conform to guidelines which relate to their formal registration as a legal entity: a company, for example, or an Industrial and Provident Association. Committees may be appointed or elected by members of the organisation, or may be a mix of both. Membership may extend simply to a small committee of interested people or be widespread.

Figure 1: An organisational classification

Key organisational characteristics

Types of organisations	Examples	Degree of professionalisation	Legal status (Formal relationship to the state)	Type of governance (Representative decision making)	Form of organisation (Organisational structure)
a) State	Quangos Councils Central government departments	Paid staff	Statutorily defined	Committees elected or appointed by the state	Formal organisation
b)	Housing associations Not-for-profit trusts		State regulated	Committees appointed by trustees or founding bodies	
c) Voluntary/non-profit organisations	Charities Advisory agencies Support organisations National campaigns				
d)	Local groups within regulated national structure Credit unions				
e) Community sector	Formal sports club Community associations Tenants' associations/Neighbourhood Watch etc	Volunteers	Legally constituted	Committees elected by membership	Formalised group
f)	Anti-Poll Tax Unions LETS Unqualified self-help support groups Bristol Care and Repair quilter's group	Activists (no staff)	Informal constitution	Informal collectives	
g) Mutual aid	Community sport — Informal literacy schemes Shared childcare — Community protection Soup kitchens		Informal rules	Group of activists	Informal group
h)	Informal care of friends, neighbours, relatives Friendship networks, reading groups	Individuals	Some conventions	Individuals	
i) Personal self-help	Squatting Allotments Carrying a security alarm/physical self-defence Non-payment of tax/bills etc	No paid staff	No formal relationship to the state	Direct decision making	Individuals Network structure

The territory *between the voluntary sector and the community sector (d)* is occupied by organisations which may relate to a formal federal voluntary sector structure at national or regional level, but operate as a network of semi-autonomous local groups. These may draw on national resources but to all intents and purposes act as local community groups, without their own paid staff. Also in this territory may lie informal or community-based associations which are becoming more formalised in response to pressures to grow and employ staff or which own a building but which do not employ staff (Marriott, 1997).

The community sector (e) has quite different organisational characteristics. Like organisations in the voluntary sector, its organisations are formally constituted. They may have a chair, secretary and treasurer, a bank account and standing orders, but they do not employ paid staff. Some of their federations may do so, but these – within our typology – would be part of the voluntary sector. Community sector organisations will usually be responsible to a committee elected by members and will involve majority control by members of their reference community.

The territory *between the community sector and the mutual aid sector (f)* is occupied by a set of groups which would include LETS and unaffiliated self-help groups. These, like community organisations, have no formal staff. They may have access to state resources (eg, community development support, sessional training, use of facilities) but they will not be funded. What distinguishes these groups from the level of organisation either side of them is that, on the one hand, they are not formally constituted but, on the other, they are still formally organised according to a recognised pattern and there is still some differentiation of tasks and responsibilities. LETS schemes, for example, have a formal structure with very clear rules, and these are organised by identifiable individuals who are responsible for carrying out or coordinating tasks.

The sector below is the heart of *the mutual aid sphere (g)*. The activities which exist within this arena will range across the full needs of disadvantaged communities: from informal sporting or leisure groups (eg, the quilters' groups described later in this report), economic exchange systems, car sharing, collective non-payment campaigns, curtain clubs/loan clubs, soup kitchens in the miners' strike (economic), community protection (safety), informal literacy schemes and learning/reading groups (education), anti-roads direct action (environment), shared childcare, informal self-help groups (care), local newsletters (communication). There are no formal rules or systems of accountability and there is no differentiation of tasks between members, but there may be informal conventions. Some groups of people can only operate in this sphere.

For example, organisations run by and for people under 18 cannot be legally constituted because people under 18 cannot be company directors or trustees.

Between the mutual aid sector and the sphere of personal activity (h) lies a sphere which is based on networks of friends, neighbours and relatives. A great deal of informal activity (including informal care) will be carried out in this sphere on a one-to-one basis and reciprocal tasks will be carried out with a less immediate expectation of payback.

Finally, at the bottom of the chart is the *sphere of personal activity (i)* which is characterised by individual and family self-help. Self help is the most direct way of resolving problems for those in most need. But while it develops from necessity it also reflects a philosophical view of the world. This was clearly articulated by Samuel Smiles in his 1859 book on 'self-help':

That which is put into us by others is always far less ours than that which we acquire by our own diligent and persevering effort. (Smiles, 1859, 1986 edn, p 194)

This analysis focuses on what people value and how they are motivated. The fact that this remark is made with reference to education lends it added significance because it suggests that having done something for ourselves we carry the knowledge forward into our lives and are able to apply it elsewhere. As such, mutual aid may be regarded not only as a response to need but as a personal and perhaps collective learning process.

It will by now be clear that, as we move down the figure, the organisational form shifts from a formal, accountable, regulated structure towards informality and from forms of organisation where ownership is clearly separate from management, operations and service use to a situation where these are completely integrated. As indicated above, our concern in this essay is with the four categories in the bottom half of the diagram. Organisations in these categories have no paid staff, no formal rules, no structure of governance or formal accountability and are largely organised as networks.

In those sectors represented by formal institutions paid workers bind organisation to professional codes of conduct, standards, guidelines for resource allocation and so on. Legal regulation binds groups to provide certain sorts of information and requires them not to do certain things. Representative forms of governance are subject to a greater threat of incorporation into the state than participative forms and are further bound into the mainstream system by the legal liability of constitutional officers. Formal and recognisable group structures are easier to control than network structures because they are visible and clearly bounded.

This means that community needs which are not provided for, funded or regulated by the state will almost inevitably be provided through forms of self-help and mutual aid. These are the most direct way of resolving problems. If people need childcare they will take it whether it is regulated or not; if people cannot pay a tax they will organise against it whether it is illegal or not; if people haven't got enough money to buy services they will use LETS schemes or even more informal exchange systems, and so on. Dependence on the state or on other formal organisations is a time-consuming, cumbersome process which may be very hit and miss, particularly for those in most need.

Notes

[1] This classification has been concerned with the spectrum that lies between the state and personal activity. But the key distinctions are as applicable to the for-profit as to the non-profit sector and the model could easily be adapted to include these.

[2] Our intention in creating this classification is not to freeze organisations into tightly defined 'sectors' but rather to demonstrate the differences between organisations that are usually treated as uniform.

[3] These boundaries are obviously permeable and we are not concerned with detailed legalistic distinctions between categories at the top end of the diagram, simply to sketch out the territory within which mutual aid is situated.

[4] Certain of their activities may be more tightly regulated, if they are carrying out work under contract to the state, but the organisation as a whole is not regulated in this way.

THREE

Informal networks and formal organisations

The extent to which formal community organisation can be formed and sustained is directly related to the capacity of communities to develop mutual aid strategies and mobilise these through networks. These processes form a fundamental part of a community's social capital – a concept coined by Coleman (1990) and Putnam (1993) to describe the networks and associations through which skills and knowledge are acquired and maintained, and which are the essential complement to financial and human capital in the development of effective organisation and governance. Tarrow and others underline the importance of personal networks in building and maintaining effective social movements (Tarrow, 1994). Opp and Gern (1993), researching the protest movement in East Germany prior to reunification, find that the mobilisation of protest was linked to friendship groups rather than membership of formal organisations.

In studying the emergence of voluntary organisations, Milofsky and Hunter (1994) argue the importance of 'background communities' as the basis for effective community organisation. Milofsky argues (1987) that the survival of individual formal organisations is less important than the development of networks which can hold 'organisational intelligence' and support a pool of local activities, which can respond to particular opportunities or challenges as they emerge, a theme which is picked up in Gilchrist and Taylor (1997) and echoed by Chanan:

> **... there is a tradition of informal and ad hoc forms of action which from time to time mobilise those people who are more aware of a problem or those who are directly involved ... they give rise to a social dynamism which fuels the action of the associations even if they are not given any organised or permanent expression. (Chanan, 1992, p 66)**

This is Putnam's 'social capital' and research on urban regeneration (Taylor, forthcoming) confirms the importance of the activity in and around the mutual aid 'sphere' in providing a foundation for engaging in more ambitious initiatives. Similarly, a recent publication by the OECD argues for a ground floor 'social economy' of informal and mutual activities as the basis for economic recovery in disadvantaged communities (Sauvage, 1996, p 14), arguing that its absence, except in criminal form, is a major problem for strategies designed to combat unemployment.

For many people in excluded communities, joining a formal organisation is not a natural thing to do. Pahl (1970) has argued that while formal organisations and formal leadership are common in middle-class communities, working-class communities are more suspicious of formalisation and the emergence of leaders. This means that counting membership of formal organisations may be a misleading way of assessing the strength of organisation and engagement in working-class communities. While committees are seen only to 'start little differences' and thus undermine solidarity, mutual aid and self-help networks strengthen solidarity, help to construct and reinforce identity, and help to create and define 'safe' environments (see also Suttles, 1972; Foster, 1995). Joining formal organisations is most likely among political activists or in the early days of a new housing estate. Incomers also join formal organisations in the hope of being able to access networks which tend to be perceived as closer to the heart of a community.

An understanding of the ties of kinship is essential to analyses of working-class communities in the past. Pahl (1970) argues that kinship ties were to the traditional working class what property is to the traditional middle class – an important source of economic security and support. Abrams (Bulmer, 1986) has distinguished between neighbours, friends and kin according to what sort of support can be expected from each. He argued that intimate caring could only be expected of the latter (perhaps because kinship provides a setting within which serial reciprocity can take place). Neighbours would be involved in crisis response and practical tasks, but to expect more of them revealed a misunderstanding of the importance of maintaining a balance in neighbouring relationships between cooperation and privacy, helpfulness and non-interference, friendliness and distance (as summarised by Allan, 1983). But in working-class communities, such as those studied by Pahl, these distinctions were overlaid by the ties of work and often religion. Thus Abrams (1980) describes traditional neighbourhoods as a densely woven world of kin, neighbours, friends and co-workers, highly localised and strongly caring within the confines of quite tightly defined relationships. The overlapping of a number of these different social relationships, and above all the relations of kinship, at local level provided the basis for local control.

However, while the dense ties and obligations of kinship are often implicit in appeals to community as a basis for caring and moral responsibility, the intensity of these relations is not always an asset, as research on child abuse demonstrates (Vinson et al, 1996; McLoyd, 1990; Salinger et al, 1983). The link between child abuse and isolation is well documented. What these authors have shown is that it is also linked to the structure of social networks. Salinger et al's study came to the conclusion that "because the limited social contact the abusive mothers had was confined primarily to their immediate families who shared many of the same values, their patterns of behaviour were probably resistant to change *and lacked the more varied input afforded by more distant parts of their network*" (Vinson et al, 1996, p 527 – our emphasis). It has been argued that the 'strong' ties commonly but not always associated with kinship and other close-knit communities may actually be less effective than a large and more diverse network of ties which are developed through other social networks. Thus, Granovetter (1973) writes of the "strength of weak ties". Weaker ties might have limits on the claims that can be made of them, but they also tend to provide indirect access to a greater diversity of resources than do stronger more socially homogenous ties (Wellman, 1979, p 1226). For, as Granovetter points out, "those to whom we are weakly tied are more likely to move in circles different from our own and will thus have access to information different from that which we receive" (1973, p 1371). In other words, diversity represents strength because it provides access to a wider variety of opportunities and perspectives on issues and problems – an idea recently taken up and developed by DEMOS (Perri 6, 1997).

Social exclusion reduces the potential for weak ties. Abrams argued (Bulmer, 1986) that the reality behind the rhetoric of close-knit community and extensive kinship attachment was often characterised by "chronic collective deprivation" and "class consciousness". Lack of contact with the outside world forces a reliance on strong ties – of kinship or other closed circles – which can be counterproductive. But the reality for many excluded communities, in the late 20th century, is that they have neither the dense overlapping networks of yesteryear nor the sparse overlapping networks required in today's world. In many mining villages, for example, the mines and allied industries, the working men's clubs, the chapels of the past have gone – eroded by economic change. Those who can, move out in search of work. There is little that actually now ties people together but the common experience of adversity and the lack of choice about where they live.

Informal networks within and beyond the neighbourhood have the capacity to fill this gap. However, they can be extremely fragile, and are not without problems. The purposes which they can fulfil, as Abrams' comparison of friends, neighbours and kin shows, may not be the intensive caring and moral control roles that characterised kinship ties, which is why in our analysis we have distinguished between mutual aid (g) and self-help based on families (i). A closer look at the way in which informal networks develop and how they are sustained is necessary if we are to assess their potential contribution to strategies which can tie people from excluded communities back into the mainstream.

FOUR

The key roles of self-help and mutual aid

Self-help and mutual aid can act as a solution to immediate problems, a springboard into mainstream society, a resource for more formal agencies, or as an alternative to aspects of mainstream society.

As a *solution* they are seen by individuals as both the most natural and effective way of organising to meet needs that more formal organisations do not address. As a *springboard* they offer routes to individual empowerment and engagement in the mainstream. As an *alternative* they may represent a preferred way of doing things – a response to the failure of more formal systems and state failure. In this section we explore the strengths and weaknesses of these three dimensions of self-help and mutual aid.

Solution

The spheres of mutual aid and self-help form a critical arena within which coping strategies are built by people in the most disadvantaged social and economic circumstances. This is because:

- they generate new possibilities for social interaction and social solidarity – this not only counters the effects of isolation but also supports identity formation and preservation;
- they can contain potential problems and prevent these from exploding and dragging down the whole community;
- they offer a sense of control over personal circumstances which dependency on the state does not;
- they support the development of skill formation by encouraging creative activity without the disincentives of state taxation which lead to poverty traps;
- they offer the possibility to generate resources from within communities where communities are explicitly excluded from mainstream resources (money, transport, access to education etc);
- they open up doors to enable people to form the 'loose networks' that may be necessary for constructing routes out of poverty and dependency (Perri 6, 1997).

Mutual aid can also be a vehicle for political action, as the experience from East Germany cited above demonstrates (Opp and Gern, 1993). The campaign of Poll Tax non-payment provides another illustration of how this works. While loose organisations – the Anti-Poll Tax Unions – were set up to coordinate some activity (these would fit in the category between the mutual aid and community sector), the vast majority of activity and communication was coordinated through parent and toddler groups, pubs and friendship networks (Burns, 1992). Without this level of organisation, the 'visible' part of the campaign would have gone nowhere. Conversely, it may also be true to say without the 'visible' hub, the invisible wheels of the campaign would not have had anything to centre around.

While mutual aid has the potential to perform all of these functions in a community, assuming that it will provide a solution where formal agency does not reach is a risky business for a number of reasons. Firstly, mutual aid and informal networks do not exist in a vacuum. In some areas (new peripheral housing estates, high rise housing developments etc) they may never have existed. Elsewhere, the very factors which have led to social and economic exclusion may also have destroyed the infrastructure on which networks were built – as in the example of the mines cited above. There is a limit to the extent to which systems of mutuality that are presumed to have existed in the past can be resurrected.

The second and third problems are interlinked. On the one hand, the very volatility and transience of mutual aid networks can limit their capacity to act as a dependable solution to exclusion. But on the other hand, once they formalise, they lose their capacity to involve people on an equal footing. The paradox for mutual aid as a solution to pressing problems is, as Michels (1915) argues, that: "organisation is both a vital condition for mobilising involvement and antithetical to its persistence". Tarrow's work on social movements comes up with similar findings. Although the cellular operations of social movements allow for a considerable extent of involvement without formalisation, ultimately movements face the risk of co-option and fragmentation (Tarrow, 1994).

A fourth problem is that, even where mutuality survives, it has, like community and networks, a 'darker' side – of exclusion and oppression. Informal networks are defined by who they exclude as well as who they include and the price of inclusion might be high. This makes them vulnerable to fragmentation and fracture. These problems are not features that can be ironed out by enlightened policy interventions. The negative qualities are the obverse of the positive qualities of mutuality. Belonging helps to define an identity for people who feel excluded, but is often based on the exclusion of others (Suttles, 1972; Foster, 1995). Networks that cater for the needs of one part of the community may be barred to others. This may be due as much to unconscious as conscious exclusion. As Chanan (1992) has argued: "Everything that disadvantages a person, either individually or because they are living in a disadvantaged neighbourhood, makes it harder for him or her to participate in group activities" (p 85).

A fifth problem is highlighted by Allan (1983), who points out that the fact people are known by their neighbours does not mean that they are constantly involved with them on an extensive and intimate basis. The word 'network' is used both to describe the contacts that a particular person may have and active reciprocal relationships between people, but it is a mistake to assume one implies the other.

Springboard

For many people in excluded communities, the primary role of self-help and mutual aid will be as a means for and beyond subsistence survival but, although it is probable that few enter into mutuality with this intention, these activities can also be the first step up a ladder of integration into mainstream society. This may involve a transition from informal exchange to more formal, paid enterprise. People may develop the skills to take them into the formal economy through developing expertise within a LETS system. People may find a route from living on the streets to mainstream housing via squatting. Childcare provided through mutual aid may enable both informal providers and users to take employment. These links are largely unrecognised and undocumented. Where they are recognised the response of the state is often to try and regulate the process.

Alternatively, self-help and mutual aid can be a route to involvement in more formal organisations. The examples which follow illustrate this:

The development of a quilters' group is an example of how informal activity can be cultivated as a route to democratic involvement. For many years Bristol Care and Repair had been trying, without success, to involve users on its management committee. The situation was not turned around as a result of a planned strategy from the organisation, but through an opportunistic piece of short-term seed funding provided (from Comic Relief) to provide sessional support and material resources for about 10 women to start up a quilting group. The women became immersed in quilting and established a very robust network through this artistic activity. As a spin-off some of the group became involved on the management committee of Bristol Care and Repair.

A tenants' association in Glasgow had been trying for years to get young people involved in their meetings. They put posters up in the local housing scheme and even tried to target specific young people but no one was interested. It was only when some members of the tenants' association (not with their tenants' association hats on) got involved in sporting activities with an informal group of young people that some of the young people began to see the potential of the tenants' association. The focus of engagement here, however, was with the sporting activity and not the tenants' association.

Both these examples show how people get involved in formal democratic decision-making forums as a result of engagement in mutual activities.

Squatting is a short-term solution to immediate need, but it becomes a springboard as a result of the stability gained from having housing. As a result, most squatters are able to find their way back into mainstream housing within five years. But squatting also illustrates how the springboard effect reinforces informal activity and makes it more viable. Thus erstwhile squatters often help to sustain the more informal activity by providing financial support for national support agencies such as the Advisory Service for Squatters. This reinforcing activity is also apparent in hitchhiking. People who have spent many years hitching lifts because they cannot afford to pay for transport, will often offer lifts to other people as soon as they have more income. This is a kind of 'long-term' reciprocity, often done out of a sense of obligation and loyalty to an idea of informal exchange.

Two issues spring to mind here. The first is that the potential for mutual aid as a springboard may be very closely related to life cycle. It is possible that people in their late teens and twenties may have a greater involvement in mutual aid activities as a springboard. In addition to their immediate need, young people are less likely to be linked into the institutions of the state and more open to alternative ways of thinking and doing things. The second is that there is a form of reciprocity at work here which is quite different to that of, say, blood donors. Titmuss' (1970) famous study of blood donors illustrated a form of reciprocity which involved people giving in the expectation that were they or their loved ones in need at some future date then they would also be provided for – a form of insurance in kind. The hitchhiking example is more closely connected to obligation and a sense that we should give something back to pay for what we have benefited from in the past.

Alternative

In some cases, individuals may see informal mutual arrangements as an alternative way of operating. Thus LETS may be seen as preferable to entering the formal economy or even as a political challenge to a society based on monetary exchange, a credit union as preferable to formal banking. Similarly, informal health initiatives may arise out of strongly held convictions that mainstream medical interventions are not likely to make individuals or society more healthy. Further toward the margins of legality, a network of skilled or semi-skilled tradespeople operating an informal referral system may find staying in the grey economy financially more viable than declaring their earnings or taking a formal job and facing the benefit trap. Or a local community may reject the response of formal justice systems which often act only after an offence has occurred and defend themselves in advance of attacks – as in the case of racial harassment.

As an alternative, mutual and informal networks build a counterculture – legal or illegal – which allows individuals to survive in a wider society which has rejected them. Squatting is one example of this, vigilantism another. But while all these activities operate in the grey areas at the margins of legality, it is important to distinguish between shades of grey. For some, mutuality may be seen as part of a social movement to change the system. Others, as in the case of criminal subcultures from street gangs to the Mafia, seek to prey on the system and would not wish to change it. Many activities fall into neither category. As Foster (1995) demonstrated, however, their solutions may involve different constructions of what is acceptable, in which levels of acceptance of benefit fraud, turning a blind eye to crime, defining certain crimes as acceptable, manipulating systems to the edges of legality, are seen as normal practice and in no way wrong. As such, they seek to 'sidestep' rather than subvert the system.

FIVE

The response of the state

For mainstream society and the state there are three possible responses to mutual aid and self-help in socially excluded areas or populations. They can be seen as compatible with more formal solutions and running in parallel with them; they can be seen as part of a continuum; or they can be seen as conflictual – a form of behaviour that cannot coexist with formal society. They may therefore by treated in one of three ways. Society may decide to do nothing about them, or tolerate them, because it keeps people quiet. Alternatively society may welcome them and actively encourage them as a resource. Thirdly, society may seek to control them, either through tax and regulation which seeks to bring them into the mainstream, or through active repression.

Tolerance

One response for the state is to assume the existence of mutual aid as a compatible system and, at the very least, to tolerate it. Much of the informal economy has been tolerated in the past, although in some cases, the pressure on benefits and welfare systems is squeezing this option. Squatting is another interesting case. Squatters do have legal rights (although these have diminished over the past decade). However, the extent of squatting in particular geographical localities has closely followed the degree to which it has been tolerated by the state. Squatting is virtually non-existent in urban areas outside London because it has received zero tolerance and in these areas may only be carried out by the homeless in the most desperate circumstances, and militant activists who see squatting as a form of defiance. In London, its incidence has risen or fallen depending on how liberal the local council is. There have been times in Lambeth, Hackney and Islington, for example, where a blind eye has been turned to squatting, when the relevant council has not had the money to do up dwellings in long-term disrepair. In the 1970s when more money was available, squats were licensed as short-life co-ops and in certain cases where houses were in very bad states of disrepair, tenancy rights were given alongside grants to do up the properties. There have been other times where riot police have been sent into council estates to evict anyone who was squatting.

As this example shows, the state's view of squatting has been confused. At different times, in different places, it has variously been seen as compatible with state activities, a staging-post and a serious moral threat. State responses to hitchhiking show the same confusion. In some countries it has been made illegal, in others (such as Britain) it is illegal on motorways. In others not only is it legal, but it forms part of a continuum of mutuality which goes from hitching to informal car-sharing, to state-supported lift schemes.

Resource

The role of mutual aid as a solution or as a foundation for formal engagement with the mainstream – a springboard for individuals – suggests that mutuality can be a resource for agencies and policy makers and needs to be actively encouraged. Since the Seebohm Report in 1968, social workers have been encouraged to see informal community networks in this way, and this was reinforced with the introduction of care management with the 1990 NHS and Community Care Act, where informal caring was seen as integral to care packages. The police force has encouraged Neighbourhood Watch schemes as a complement to their more formal intervention. A number of authors, building on the social capital debate, have also underlined the need for community networks and informal activity as the basis for more formal engagement with the economy (eg, OECD, 1996), with democracy (Hirst, 1994) and with policy developments which increasingly seek community participation and partnership (Taylor, 1995; Wilson and Charlton, 1997).

But this assumes that informal and formal systems are at least compatible and, further, that they operate along a continuum. The evidence for this is mixed.

Janet Foster's work on crime suggests a complex relationship, but one that is ultimately symbiotic. She argues that informal responses can give residents control over fear of crime: "crime need not in itself be debilitating if residents feel they can challenge and confront it by utilising both informal and formal control mechanisms" (Foster, 1995, p 565). Informal networks help in a number of ways: they define what is seen as threatening and what can be tolerated or even encouraged as normal practice – 'how most East Enders survive'; they neutralise fear by encouraging face-to-face contact and reducing the 'fear of strangers'; they offer 'opportunities for informal surveillance'; and they offer a means to informal conflict resolution. Foster reports considerable resistance to formal intervention in these functions – including Neighbourhood Watch: "tenants favoured informal conflict resolution, avoiding official sanctions if at all possible, and rarely respected official sanctions if imposed"(p 577). Indeed, local people saw the way in which formal systems formalised and defined problems as counterproductive. On the other hand, Foster reports that the informal system depended to some extent on the 'backstop' of more formal intervention: "When the formal mechanisms of control were working effectively on the estate, tenants knew that these channels could be utilised if informal sanctions failed or where a mixture of formal and informal sanctions seemed most appropriate" (p 579). When a community policing system was withdrawn from the areas she studied, informal control systems – which had kept this system very much at arm's-length – broke down.

Others warn that the assumption of a seamless web between mutuality and formal systems is misconceived (Hoch and Hemmens, 1987). Indeed, there may be fundamental contradictions in the roles that each play. The field of community care provides an example. Informal care depends on reciprocity and the character of personal relationships; professional systems are supposed to be detached.

The community and self-help literatures highlight a further problem where policy makers attempt to use mutuality as a resource. In the economic field, Offe and Heinze (1992) find that the most successful examples of moneyless exchange are small and based on the 'solidarity capital' possessed by those people who belong to more or less tightly knit social groups: "Once the limits of that particular social frame have been reached, the very factor that was such a potent help at the beginning turns into a barrier to further growth" (p 167). Thus, while informal mutual aid networks may act as a springboard for individuals and a 'background community' from which more formal organisations can emerge – a process which outsiders can encourage – it may be dangerous for outsiders to try and 'grow' these networks themselves into more formal organisations.

Whatever the arguments for pulling informal mutual aid and self-help networks into more formal arrangements, therefore, there are also costs. Attempts to co-opt informal care fail to acknowledge its fragility and can endanger its social integrity.

Wilson (1995) recommends that while resources need to be put in to support self-help groups, this should be done by supporting intermediary organisations, which can play a catalytic, nurturing, or support role, a view shared by Wann (1995). This might include resource support (eg, access to space, equipment, expertise), providing publicity, or simply putting people in touch with each other, but both authors are adamant that such groups must be left to determine their own direction and priorities. The Poll Tax example (see p 16) provides another example of the value of this arm's-length support, although in somewhat different circumstances.

While attempts to intervene or co-opt mutuality are likely to lead to its destruction, a feature of this kind of activity may be its regenerative nature. Thus new informal organisations will often spring up as fast as their predecessors are co-opted, because they fulfil a fundamental role for local communities and for society at large. Where this leaves the co-opted organisation is uncertain, but co-option is likely to prejudice both its legitimacy and effectiveness.

One more point is worth making in this section. It is not only the state that seeks to formalise mutuality. Offe and Heinze (1992) point to the tendency for the market to make services that have traditionally been informally exchanged for free into commodities which are for sale. This inevitably devalues the skills involved in own work. This commodification can discourage people from acquiring or using these skills or from operating informally in this sphere.

Regulation and repression

Some informal and mutual aid networks will be seen as more threatening by society. The obvious examples are criminal and subcriminal networks on the one hand, controlled by policing and an increasing emphasis on zero tolerance, and vigilante activities on the other. But as the grey areas of the economy and the welfare system are more rigorously policed, more benign mutual solutions are increasingly vulnerable to economic and safety regulation. Official systems are threatened by those who operate on the margins and place considerable obstacles in the way of transition from the informal to the formal economy – not least the benefit trap. The state often sees the type of activities that we have described as a threat because:

- they tend not to be very visible to those involved and are thus not seen to be accountable to society as a whole – this lack of public visibility makes them difficult to control;
- neither mutual aid nor self-help allocate resources according to rules or criteria – they largely operate on a 'first come first served' basis, or

as 'action in direct response to need' – this appears contradictory to institutions which must appear to act consistently;

- there is a tendency within many of the institutions of the state to believe that anything (including the voluntary sector) which organises outside the state has the potential to turn against the state – for this reason mutual aid and self-help activities may not be trusted;
- there are genuine tensions between allowing informal care and guarding against abuse.

Nonetheless, Offe and Heinze (1992) argue that government policies have increasingly taken an interest in activities located in this no man's land, such as illicit work, the informal economy, self-help and own work, and so on, for three reasons: in order to look for ways of escape from the bottlenecks caused by crises in public finances; to overcome the functional weaknesses of bureaucratically organised state social services; to open up possible lines of escape for 'superfluous' sections of the labour market.

As a result, it seems that many of the grey areas in social and economic life have been placed under increasing scrutiny and scrutiny brings with it increasing regulation. Mutual aid activities that were once tolerated as a solution run the risk of being defined as outside the system and either become unavailable as a means of survival or become a source of tension between the community and the rest of society.

Thus, a woman may decide to look after some of her friends' children as a way of making a little money. For her friends, this frees them to work or get involved in other activities. But she runs the risk of being regarded as in breach of regulation – even if she does it for nothing. A group may decide to set up a LETS scheme. But they may find that a benefits officer regards them as being unavailable for work, that business complains of unfair (untaxed) competition or that the Inland Revenue are watching their development closely, because the system sees what they are doing as untaxed exchange. Certainly in the social care field, the increase in regulations and the requirement for qualifications can make it more difficult for people to engage in caring, childcare or even cooking tasks in the grey area between formal and informal activity, thus creating another formidable barrier to those who wish to move from one to the other. In a recent study, one voluntary sector manager bemoaned the fact that women (in this particular case) who had been cooking and looking after children all their lives were now being required to have qualifications and submit to safety standards defined for much more formal circumstances (Taylor et al, 1995).

Community solutions often find themselves operating in the grey areas at the margins of legality – because it works. This leads the state at best to be ambivalent about the activities within the mutual aid sector. Where it is prepared to tolerate mutual aid it will usually try to control it and in doing so it will often destroy it. To deliver support without intervention, the state will need to learn to live with contradictions and inconsistencies, accepting that the zone between desperation and assimilation into the mainstream may involve organising principles the state may not wish to condone or even acknowledge. The pay-off for this is that large numbers of people will be able to create solutions to their own problems, solutions which the state is not in a position to provide.

SIX

Some lessons for policy makers

A delicate balancing act is needed if mutuality is to be encouraged without being incorporated or suppressed. On the one hand, policy makers may experience mutual aid activities and networks as intangible, volatile, and small scale, rising and falling as required and they may therefore see them only as an elusive and frustrating resource to work with. On the other hand, if they do work with them, they run the danger of distorting them. In resolving this tension, it is important to understand that mutual aid networks operate within larger communities. And it is their relationship with the larger community which may prove crucial. On the one hand, as Milofsky and Hunter (1994) argue, mutual aid and community networks may prove a springboard for more formal organisations and a 'Greek chorus' to hold these more formal organisations accountable. On the other, these larger communities can compensate for the transitoriness of mutual aid networks by providing an environment for 'serial reciprocity' – help offered at one stage in a person's life may be paid back at a later stage – and thus providing a background of trust and common expectations in which reciprocity can flourish. Churches often play a similar role (Harris, 1995). Thus, where networks operate within a dependable 'community' setting, they can operate at optimal levels and may reconstitute or be reconfigured over time.

If there is intervention, therefore, it is most appropriately targeted at the more formal community sector as the appropriate mediating body. This conclusion is supported by Wann (1995) and Wilson (1995), who both recommend that while self-help groups do not need direct resources from the state, there is an important role for intermediaries – organisations which act as development and resource centres and can provide support at arm's length, articulating mutualism into the continuum of social action that we have suggested above (see Figure 1). It is also supported by our earlier examples of mutual aid as a springboard to organisation.

The social movement model offers a similar way forward. Tarrow (1994) describes social movements as "an interlocking network of small groups, social networks and the connections between them" (p 57). This model also allows them to relapse into informal networks at times of demobilisation. He cites the women's movement as an example of networks sustained over a long period, which have allowed former activists to emerge decades later, when the opportunity has arisen. But he is aware of the dangers of "the inevitable co-option of movements" and looks in the end for a delicate balance between "suffocating the power in movement by providing too much organisation and leaving it to spin off uselessly through the tyranny of decentralisation". His reference to the need for social relays or mobilising structures which link networks to one another and activate dormant links, underlines again the need to support mutual aid indirectly through mediating mechanisms rather than attempting to intervene directly.

At its best, a community development approach can act in this way (Gilchrist and Taylor, 1997), actively encouraging the formation of a diverse range of mutual aid networks so as to make the overall pattern of mutual aid more inclusive and linking people into and across informal networks (Gilchrist, 1995). While community development workers run the danger of acting as gatekeepers of privileged pathways to power (Clegg, 1989) rather than social relays, there is some evidence that mutual aid networks facilitated by outside professionals can be more inclusive than those which grow from within the community (CDJ, 1996). But outside intervention requires a very delicate balancing act, if the balance between formalisation and flexibility, exclusion and inclusion is to be maintained and incorporation avoided.

If mutual aid is to act as a springboard for people in excluded communities, therefore, we need to learn the lessons highlighted by the work of Granovetter, Wellman, Abrams and Pahl, reported in Chapter 3. Tarrow argues that "the ties of homogenous groups are inimical to broader mobilisation. Weak ties among social networks that were not unified were much stronger than the strongest ties of workbench or family" (Tarrow, 1994, p 60). This is a message that has recently been picked up again by Perri 6 (1997) who argues that the kinds of 'community' that policy should seek to encourage are those which are based on a broad network of loose ties, rather than the more conventional understanding of community as a tight network of strong ties based on family and kinship. In essence the greater number and the greater diversity of ties that people have the more likely that they will generate opportunity. Conversely, in a 'drawbridge' society, which seeks to cut itself off from those who have become marginalised, exclusion becomes a self-fulfilling prophecy.

SEVEN

Conclusion

In this essay, we have identified a 'sphere' of social organisation characterised by self-help and mutual aid – a 'sector' which is quite distinct from either the voluntary or the community sectors. The activities of this 'sphere of activity' are characterised by the absence of paid staff, informal rules, direct forms of decision making and a network structure of organisation. This distances them from the control of the state and other outside interests. This 'sphere' of activity can act as a solution, springboard and alternative in current policy. In all of these forms it is a fundamental part of the fabric of society. It can ensure innovation and diversity precisely because it operates outside the uniformity which results from state regulation and a democratic system which only legitimises majority decisions.

It is because mutual aid and self-help can provide direct and practical solutions to immediate need that this sector is so vital a response to social exclusion. While there is evidence of such activities in both middle-class and low-income communities, however, they have a different significance in each. For middle-class communities mutual aid and self-help may be seen as one strand in a web of choices. For people who are socially excluded and on low incomes they are often the only way of coping where there is no alternative safety net.

In fostering this resource, policy makers should bear in mind the following.

- The links between sectors are crucial. Without a careful consideration of self-help and mutual aid, policy directed at the community and voluntary sectors and the state will be fundamentally flawed.
- Having acknowledged this, policy interventions are extremely difficult in this area. Mutual aid can easily be destroyed by attempts to incorporate. The most effective interventions are likely to come through support for mediating organisations in the community and the creation of a 'benign' environment.
- The more communities become cut off, the more likely they are to lose the loose ties which allow people to find and create opportunities to rejoin the mainstream. Old-fashioned ideas of tight, self-sufficient communities are no longer relevant to today's society.

• The differences in organisational structure, ideology, form of accountability and so on which characterise mutual aid and self-help need to be tolerated by mainstream society, and policy makers need to develop pragmatic policy frameworks which can live with the inherent contradictions.

Finally, it is important to remind ourselves that what on the face of it may seem small-scale activities combine to form a huge web of social and economic activities which exist outside of state regulation and form the bedrock of our society. For the future, we need to find ways of mapping the extent of mutual aid activities and explore how links are built from the sphere of mutual aid up through more formal organisations to the state and back in order *not* to control them but to understand how the diversity which they represent can be accommodated in a way which plays to their strengths.

References

Abrams, P. (1980) 'Social change, social networks and neighbourhood care', *Social Work Service*, vol 22, pp 12-23.

Allan, G. (1983) 'Informal networks of care: issues raised by Barclay', *British Journal of Social Work*, vol 13, pp 417-33.

Bulmer, M. (1986) *Neighbours: The work of Philip Abrams*, Cambridge: Cambridge University Press.

Burns, D. (1992) *Poll Tax rebellion,* Edinburgh: AK Press.

Chanan, G. (1992) *Out of the shadows: Local community action in the European Community,* Dublin: EFILWIC.

Clegg, S. (1989) *Frameworks of power*, London: Sage.

Coleman, J. S. (1990) *Foundations of social theory*, Cambridge, MA: Harvard University Press.

Davidson, M., Redshaw, J. and Mooney, A. (1997) *The role of DIY in maintaining owner-occupied stock*, Bristol: The Policy Press.

Field, F. (1996) *Stakeholder welfare*, London: IEA Health and Welfare Unit.

Foster, J. (1995) 'Informal control and community crime prevention', *British Journal of Criminology*, vol 35, no 4, pp 563-83.

Gilchrist, A. (1995) *Community development and networking*, London: Community Development Foundation.

Gilchrist, A. and Taylor, M. (1987) 'Community networking: developing strength through diversity', in P. Hoggett (ed) *Contested communities: Experiences, struggles, policies*, Bristol: The Policy Press.

Granovetter, M. (1973) 'The strength of weak ties', *American Journal of Sociology*, vol 78, no 6, pp 1360-80.

Harris, M. (1995) 'Quiet care: welfare work and religious congregations', *Journal of Social Policy*, vol 24, no 1, pp 53-71.

Hirst, P. (1994) *Associative democracy*, Cambridge: Polity Press.

Hoch, C. and Hemmens, G. (1987) 'Linking informal and informal help: conflict along the continuum of care', *Social Service Review*, September, pp 432-46.

McLoyd,V.C. (1990) 'The impact of economic hardship on black families and children: psychological distress, parenting and socio-emotional development', *Child Development*, vol 61, pp 311-46.

Marriott, P. (1997) *Forgotten resources? The role of community buildings in strengthening local communities*,York: Joseph Rowntree Foundation.

Michels, R. (1915; reprinted 1962) *Political parties*, New York: Free Press.

Milofsky, C. (1987) 'Neighbourhood-based organisations: a market analogy', in W.W. Powell (ed) *The non profit sector: A research handbook*, New Haven:Yale University Press.

Milofsky, C. and Hunter, A. (1994) 'Where nonprofits come from: a theory of organisational emergence', Report presented to the Association for Research on Nonprofit Organisations and Voluntary Action, San Francisco, October.

Mulgan, G. and Landry, C. (1995) *The other invisible hand*, London: DEMOS.

OECD (1996) *Reconciling economy and society: Towards a plural economy*, Paris: OECD.

Offe, C. and Heinze, R.G. (1992) *Beyond employment*, Cambridge: Polity Press.

Opp, K.-D. and Gern, C. (1993) 'Dissident groups, personal networks and spontaneous co-operation: the East German revolution of 1989', *American Sociological Review*, vol 58, pp 659-80.

Pahl, R. (1970) *Patterns of urban life*, London: Longman.

Paton, R. (1989) 'The social economy: value-based organisations in the wider society', in J. Batsleer, C. Cornforth and R. Paton (eds) *Issues in voluntary and non-profit management*, Wokingham: Addison-Wesley.

Perri 6 (1997) 'The power to bind and loose: tackling network poverty', London: DEMOS.

Putnam, R. (1993) *Making democracy work: Civic traditions in modern Italy*, Princeton, NJ.: Princeton University Press.

Salinger, S., Kaplan, S. and Artesnyeff, C. (1983) 'Mothers' personal social networks and child maltreatment', *Journal of Abnormal Psychology*, vol 92, no 1, pp 68-76.

Sauvage, P. (1996) 'Summary', in OECD, *Reconciling economy and society: Towards a plural economy*, Paris: OECD.

Smiles. S. (1859; 1986 edn) *Self-help*, Harmondsworth: Penguin.

Suttles, G. (1972) *The social construction of community*, Chicago: University of Chicago Press.

Tarrow, S. (1994) *Power in movement: Social movements, collective action and politics*, Cambridge: Cambridge University Press.

Taylor, M. (1995) *Unleashing the potential: Bringing residents to the centre of estate regeneration*, York: Joseph Rowntree Foundation.

Taylor, M. (forthcoming) 'Achieving community participation: the experience of resident involvement in urban regeneration in the UK', in D. Warburton (ed) *Community and sustainable development: Participation in the future*, World Wildlife Fund.

Taylor, M., Langan, J. and Hoggett, P. (1995) *Encouraging diversity: Voluntary and private organisations in community care*, Aldershot: Arena.

Titmuss, R. (1970) *The gift relationship: From human blood to social policy*, Harmondsworth: Penguin.

Vinson, T., Baldry, E. and Hargreaves, J. (1996) 'Neighbourhoods, networks and child abuse', *British Journal of Social Work*, vol 26, pp 523-43.

Wann, M. (1995) *Building social capital: Self-help in the twenty-first century welfare state*, London: Institute for Public Policy Research.

Wellman, B. (1979) 'The community question: the intimate networks of East Yorkers', *American Journal of Sociology*, vol 84, no 5, pp 1201-31.

Wilson, A. and Charlton, K. (1997) *Making partnerships work: A practical guide for the public, private, voluntary and community sectors*, York: York Publishing Services.

Wilson, J. (1995) *Two worlds: Self-help groups and professionals*, Birmingham: British Association of Social Workers.